Original title:
The Life You Want (But Can't Find)

Copyright © 2025 Creative Arts Management OÜ
All rights reserved.

Author: Elias Marchant
ISBN HARDBACK: 978-1-80566-143-6
ISBN PAPERBACK: 978-1-80566-438-3

Secrets of a Solitary Star

In a galaxy, far away, it sighs,
A star on its own, with big, twinkly eyes.
It dreams of a partner, a cosmic delight,
But no one arrives, just meteors in flight.

Each night it whispers to lonely old comets,
'Throw me a line, I'm tired of the promises!'
Yet the comets just giggle and dance in the void,
'You twinkle alone, because you've enjoyed!'

The star spins in circles, in glittery jest,
'Maybe I'll date a black hole, at best!'
But the black hole just grumbles, 'I'm busy today,'
And the star pouts, 'Why must you all stray?'

So it hosts a big party, with planets in tow,
They drink cosmic punch, put on a good show.
Yet every good time ends with a sigh,
As the star tosses confetti, then wonders "Oh, why?"

Alone but still sparkling, it beams with a grin,
'Life's best when you're solo, let chaos begin!'
The lessons are plenty in the vast, starry dome,
Sometimes the best journeys are journeys alone.

Hues of Happiness Yet Unseen

In a box of crayons, I've found my dreams,
But the broken ones are bursting at the seams.
I asked the sun to paint my skies,
Yet it's stuck in traffic, oh what a surprise!

I wear mismatched socks, that's my style,
Chasing rainbows, just a little while.
With coffee stains on my hopes and schemes,
Life plays tricks, or so it seems!

The Balancing Act of Yearning

A tightrope walker with pizza in hand,
Dreams wobble wildly, isn't life grand?
I juggle wishes like a circus clown,
But my red nose makes me fall down!

Chasing my goals in roller skates,
I trip on success, it waits and waits.
Floating on hopes, oh the things I might do,
If only my cat didn't steal my shoe!

Surreal Landscapes of the Soul

I wander through valleys made of cake,
Where gummy bears swim in a chocolate lake.
The trees wear hats and dance at night,
While marshmallows giggle, oh what a sight!

A cloud whispers secrets, sticky and sweet,
It told me to dance with two left feet.
With a grin like a fox, in this place I wander,
Chasing dreams like a kid, I can't help but ponder!

When Wishes Whisper Back

I wished on a star, but it turned to cheese,
Now I'm plotting how to get more with ease.
When wishes mutter like a grumpy cat,
I join them for tea, how 'bout that?

They spoke of dreams hidden under the bed,
So I checked, but found only dust instead.
With hiccups of hope, I'm still askin' why,
The universe laughs as I reach for the sky!

Longing for What Eludes

I dream of a castle made of cheese,
With rivers of chocolate, oh, what a tease!
Instead, I'm stuck with my snack-sized chips,
Daydreaming of gourmet food on my trips.

My heart craves a yacht, oh what a delight,
But I'm stuck with my paddle, it's such a fright.
"Adventure awaits!" my friends often boast,
While I search for my socks, a mundane ghost.

Fragments of a Distant Horizon

I wander the mall in my mismatched shoes,
Browsed through a store selling dreams I can't choose.
Called a 'life coach', but he sells me a pen,
"To sketch out your woes" — I should've said when!

The horizon's shimmering, yet stays out of reach,
I signed up for salsa but learned how to screech.
Chasing perfection feels like a race,
But I'm busy tripping on my own shoelace.

The Quest for Invisible Splendor

I seek glittering gold in a world made of dust,
Wishing my failures could turn into rust.
Life's a confetti storm swept by a breeze,
And I'm stuck with a ticket for 'Just sit and freeze.'

They say life's a movie, but I'm stuck on mute,
Plus popcorn for dinner feels less than astute.
I chase all the stars, but I trip on the ground,
Wanna ride in the sky, instead, I just pound.

Silent Cries of the Heart

I sing to the toaster, it burns every bread,
Hoping it helps me escape this dread.
A prince on a horse? More like a frog,
Not a wave of magic, just a horrible fog.

The fridge hums a tune, but no food's in sight,
My plans for a banquet could start quite a fight.
In dreams, I dance on a cloud made of fluff,
While I trip over laundry — how's that for tough?

Chasing Illusions in the Mist

I chased my dreams like a cat with a mouse,
Yet tripped on my laces, fell flat on the grouse.
The fog rolled in thick, made sure I was lost,
It's hard to find joy when you're counting the cost.

I don't know the route, the map's all askew,
With signs pointing left, and I'm still heading blue.
A white rabbit giggles, as I fall through the haze,
It seems even magic can't fix my malaise.

In Search of Unwritten Chapters

With a pen in my pocket, I search for the plot,
But all I can find is a half-eaten scone, and a lot.
The manuscript's blank, my coffee's gone cold,
Oh, where are the stories that should've been told?

I scribble a line, but it turns out to rhyme,
About how my sock drawer needs a good climb.
I chase after plot twists and characters neat,
But they always escape on their own two feet!

Pathways to the Unseen

I wandered the paths that were paved with good cheer,
Only to find squirrels that laughed at my fear.
The road that I picked took a twist in the night,
And suddenly I was in quite a strange fright.

A sign says "This way" with arrows galore,
But they point to a bakery (like I need more!)
I followed the crumbs until they ran dry,
And there I was left, with no pie to supply!

Unraveled Threads of Aspiration

I knitted my hopes with a yarn full of dreams,
But somehow it tangled and fell at the seams.
Each stitch was a vision, a spark of delight,
Yet here I am sitting, with knots in my sight.

The needle went missing, the fabric ran wild,
Like a chaotic toddler, my plans were defiled.
With a sprinkle of laughter, I embrace the loss,
Because who needs a tapestry when you're a boss?

Longing for a Different Sky

I dream of clouds that shape like fries,
Or sunsets painted with big pink pies.
A rainbow dance with silly hats,
Where unicorns play with friendly cats.

But here I am, the laundry's near,
With socks that vanish, oh dear, oh dear!
My dreams fly high while I just sigh,
Trapped in a world where fuzzballs cry.

Threads of Tomorrow's Tapestry

I weave my dreams with spaghetti strands,
Making potpourris with my own hands.
Bots and robots, bold and fine,
While I eat ice cream, sipping on wine.

But socks and chores claim all my time,
Life's more of a circus, without the prime.
I stitch my hopes with tangled yarn,
Wishing for more laughs, less forlorn.

Keyholes to Unknown Futures

I peek through keyholes, oh what a sight,
A world with disco balls, oh so bright!
Planes made of candy, clouds of cheese,
But here I am, dodging all the fleas.

I dream of adventures in candy land,
While my toast burns, and it's looking bland.
Life's a puzzle, missing a piece,
I giggle, wishing for sweet release.

Unwritten Pages of Desire

I've got blank pages in my notebook sky,
Staring at lists that just make me cry.
To write a tale of daring flair,
While hunting for snacks, oh, please beware.

I scribble notes, a pirate's quest,
But end up finding just my old vest.
Each line I pen is a funny fight,
Wishing for magic, not just delight.

Fleeting Moments

In the fridge, there's a pizza
It promises joy, but it's cold
Took a bite, I fell to my knees
How did dinner turn into gold?

The cat steals my pillow each night
As I chase dreams, a soft purr.
He plots world dominion with glee,
While I strive for a gourmet burger.

My shoes squeak with every bold step,
They dance like they're at a ball.
Yet every leap feels like a misstep,
As I trip on my hopes, I just fall.

Endless Longings

With coffee in hand, I search for bliss,
A sock thief wearing a sly grin.
My brain whirls in an endless abyss,
Where did I hide that last spoon again?

Dreams come like butterflies, light and frail,
But land on my nose, then take flight.
I wave goodbye to each glorious tale,
As chores call me back from their height.

The laundry's a mountain, daunting and high,
It whispers tales of adventures afar.
If only the socks were in pairs to comply,
I'd ride on the back of a rainbow star.

The Serenade of Lost Possibilities.

I planned a party with flair and zest,
But only two friends came to stay.
We played charades, and all confessed,
It was a weird game of 'who's in dismay?'

The cake collapsed, a true work of art,
My cat was the judge, purring away.
With forks in hand, we played our part,
As frosting became the game of the day.

Outside pigeons coo like lost souls,
They chat about dreams in flight.
While I contemplate my intricate goals,
They just want crumbs to delight.

Chasing Shadows of Desire

I chase a shadow, thinking it's gold,
Only to find it's the dog's old bone.
Our dreams often leave us feeling so bold,
But they toss us like leaves, and we moan.

My mirror laughs as I strut with style,
Expecting fortune to follow my lead.
But my hair has plans to revile,
And my shirt is an accidental breed.

The mailman brings bills instead of fortune,
Each day it's like winning the lottery—sort of!
If only I could create a cartoon scene,
With money growing on the green cabbages of skewer.

Dreams Beyond the Horizon

With stars in my eyes, I reach for the sky,
Imagining fame, a grandiose scheme.
But I trip over furniture, oh my!
My ambitions take flight, then it's a dream.

A dance in the moonlight, how cool it would be,
But I've stepped on a cat, not quite the plan.
As I leap like a fox, wild and free,
Turns out I prefer a quiet lifespan.

The universe whispers, 'Just take that chance',
But who knew it meant wearing mismatched socks?
So I'll sip my tea and try a slow dance,
With my dreams still tangled in cozy blocks.

Cravings of the Untrodden Path

I dream of sheep on pogo sticks,
And llamas in cowboy hats,
But here I am with dirty dishes,
Instead of chatting with the cats.

I chase after pies that float like clouds,
With legs so skinny, they run away,
While unicorns tap dance on rainbows,
I'm stuck in line for stale parfaits.

My heart's set on a disco llama,
But I'm on hold with customer care,
They say my dreams are out of reach,
I just want glitter in my hair.

I map my routes on spaghetti strands,
With meatball towns and sauce-filled seas,
Instead, I'm counting paperclips,
As they shimmy like they're at a tease.

Echoes of a Silent Song

I hum a tune of jelly beans,
That bounce around in funky shoes,
But every note's a silent scream,
A concert for the nightly blues.

I dance with ghosts of bad ideas,
Wearing socks of mismatched flair,
While disco balls just float on by,
I trip while trying to declare.

The symphony of socks and spoons,
Plays softly in my living room,
But all I hear's the whirr of chores,
And dust bunnies dance with gloom.

I'd trade my box of dreary dreams,
For one small tune of perfect cheer,
Yet all I get's a kazoo sound,
While pizza's sliding down the pier.

Reflections in a Broken Mirror

I glance at shards of dreams gone mad,
With wobbly waves of fate's design,
My face looks like a sad old cat,
Just missing out on homemade wine.

I spy a hero in the glass,
With capes made out of sandwich wraps,
He takes a sip of fizzy floor,
And yells, 'My kingdom for some naps!'

The mirror showed me pizza crusts,
That danced like they were free of sin,
But then it turned into a toast,
To cheer my many woes within.

I'd paint a smile on all my frowns,
With sprinkles and a side of cream,
Instead, I'm stuck with fragmented thoughts,
That weave a most absurd machine.

The Canvas of Untold Dreams

I splatter colors from a can,
Hoping pastel clouds will grow,
But end up with a messy hand,
Creating art that's just for show.

With brush strokes done in bubble gum,
I try to paint a sunlit day,
But my ideas float away fast,
Like kittens trying to learn ballet.

I craft a world of cheese and wine,
With popcorn trees and fizzy streams,
Yet all I have is crayon drawings,
Of my pet's most laughable dreams.

So here I splash in puddles wide,
With laughter echoing through the seams,
Creating joy with every glide,
In this odd gallery of dreams.

The Mirage of Perfect Moments

Chasing rainbows, I trip on my shoes,
Dancing with shadows, I still seem to lose.
The ice cream truck's music plays in my head,
But here I am, stuck in a life that I dread.

I scroll through my feed, everyone's bliss,
While I'm over here just dreaming of this.
A sip of the fountain of happiness pure,
But where's the recipe? I can't find the cure.

A Needle in a Haystack Heart

Searching for love like it's made out of gold,
But all I find is someone who's cold.
My heart's a lost sock in a dryer of fate,
Twisting and turning—oh, when will I mate?

They say there's a soulmate out there for me,
But I've got a cat and she's quite the spree.
I'll take a wild guess—the one's in a tree,
Or maybe they're hiding, drinking tea with a bee.

Yearning Shadows at Dusk

The clock chimes softly, it's nearly too late,
Tangled in dreams that just won't abate.
I paint with my wishes, but the colors won't blend,
It's a canvas of chaos that just won't mend.

I sleep on my hopes like a blanket of dust,
While my neighbor's lawn gnome collects all my trust.
My shadows keep laughing, they're bold and precise,
The future seems dim, and yet I hear mice.

Ghosts of Ambitions Past

Once I had dreams as big as the moon,
Now I just seek where the remote went too soon.
My plans haunt my mind, like an ex left behind,
Whispering sweet nothings no longer aligned.

With each cup of coffee, I plot my comeback,
But the couch is too comfy—I'll just stay on track.
The ghosts hold the door, they chuckle and sigh,
As I drift off to sleep with ambition awry.

The Bridge Between Then and Now

I skated on memories, my shoelaces tied,
Fell into puddles where yesterdays hide.
The bridge creaks loudly, a joke on my knees,
Except for the ducks, they float with such ease.

Each step is a waltz with ghosts in a line,
They giggle and whisper, 'Come dance and you'll shine.'
But I trip on my laces, they just roll their eyes,
Life's punchline is clever, but oh, what a surprise!

Ribbons of Solitude

In a box marked 'lonely,' I found a bright bow,
Wrapped around the silence, a gift I outgrew.
I tried to unpin it, but it tied me up tight,
Dancing with shadows, my partner for night.

Thought I'd invite joy, just a little more fun,
But joy showed up late, all tangled and spun.
We laughed 'til we cried at the mess on the floor,
Ribbons of solitude, a confetti galore.

Moments that Slipped Away

I chased after seconds with a butterfly net,
They flutter and giggle, oh, what a duet.
Some flashed by quickly, like cars on a track,
While others just lingered, then vanished—oh, whack!

The minutes are tricksters, they dance like they're free,
Stealing my punchlines—how silly of me!
But in every lost instant, a giggle remains,
Like socks in the dryer, they dance in my brain.

The Unraveled Thread of Existence

My tapestry's fraying, with threads coming loose,
I tie and I knot them, this yarn's quite obtuse.
Each pull's a new chuckle, each spin's a new tale,
Rabbits in hats, yet I still seem to fail.

I tug on my worries, they dangle and sway,
A circus of thoughts in a grand cabaret.
But every old fray leads to laughter again,
In the quilt of my chaos, I'm happy—amen!

Flickering Hopes in Twilight

In the shade of dreams that dance,
They play charades with fate's last chance.
A rubber chicken on my wall,
It cackles loudly through it all.

I shoo away the pesky doubt,
With silly hats, I laugh and shout.
A jester's crown, I wear with glee,
While chasing shadows endlessly.

Each wish a bubble, bright and round,
Popped by a cat that's gained a pound.
In twilight's glow, my heart does leap,
As dirt bike dreams in puddles creep.

With starry eyes, I wave goodbye,
To parades of donuts in the sky.
What's laughter worth without the fun?
Just sippy cups that weigh a ton.

When Wishes Wear Thorns

Once I sought a golden prize,
With sparkly dreams and hopeful eyes.
Instead, I found a prickly bush,
Teasing me with a funny hush.

A unicorn in a coffee shop,
Serves lattes topped with lollipop.
Yet every sip, a pie in the face,
Clowns juggle joy in this funny place.

Each wish I cast, like paper planes,
Sailed through storms, made of silly chains.
Their laughter echoed, loud and clear,
While I just dreamed of venturing near.

With cap and bells, I prance around,
In spinny chairs with squeaky sound.
For what's a thorn without a quirk?
Just ribbons where the giggles lurk.

Map of the Heart's Longing

I charted paths on pizza maps,
With pepperoni score of mishaps.
A compass spins, it's lost its way,
In search of dreams that play all day.

With coffee dreams in socks that mismatch,
I trip on laughs, an endless batch.
Each journey starts with a silly rhyme,
Yet ends in knots, all in good time.

A treasure marked with X's bold,
Leads to a box of rubber mold.
It overflows with quirky toys,
And jiggly worms that bring such joys.

Still wandering where the giggles grow,
In fields of giggles, I'll gladly go.
For what is longing without a jest?
A paper boat on a duck's new quest.

Threads of Illusion

I wove a quilt of dreams so bright,
With threads of laughter, day and night.
But as I stitched, they turned to yarn,
A fashion faux pas, slightly worn.

A scarf of wishes, oh so long,
Draped over hopes that slipped along.
In search of warmth, a ticklish breeze,
I chased the sun through leafy trees.

The fabric of my goals unraveled,
As juggling clowns just talent traveled.
Each thread that pulled, a giggle bled,
Creating art from silly dread.

In this wild weave, I twirl and spin,
Crafting joy from where I've been.
For in the chaos, I can see,
The beauty threads weave whimsically.

Flickers of an Elusive Star

In the fridge, my dreams get cold,
They scream for ice cream, bold and old.
I chase them down with socks and shoes,
But find they hide, like stains on blues.

Through messy rooms and cluttered nights,
I search for joy in silly flights.
A cereal box, it plays the part,
Of guiding me to my lost heart.

I wander paths of giggles and cake,
But all I find is a silly mistake.
With every trip, I end in jest,
My aspirations take an endless rest.

Yet here I stand, with laughter rife,
Sipping on the fun of life.
For though the star is hard to catch,
The joy in trying is quite a match.

Miles to Go Before I'm Home

I set out on a quest for gold,
With maps that quite simply fold.
In search of happiness, clear and bright,
I end up lost before the night.

The GPS says, 'You're still not there,'
While I'm bumping into bushes bare.
I wave at squirrels, they mock my plight,
The road ahead just feels too tight.

There's coffee brewing in my dreams,
But all I brew are half-sweet schemes.
With every sip of missed delight,
I laugh at fate, it feels so right.

Yet every mile brings fails to see,
I'll dance with all my fallacies.
For home is where the puns unfold,
In every story that I've told.

Starlit Roads to Nowhere

They say the stars will guide my way,
But all I see is a light display.
I follow trails of cosmic fun,
Yet end up lost with every pun.

My nights are filled with playful schemes,
As shadows pull me into dreams.
A comet swings, it steals my hat,
While aliens giggle on my mat.

Each twinkling light a cheeky tease,
Daring me to find some ease.
But as I stroll these sparkling paths,
I trip on laughter, earn their wrath.

Could it be that nowhere's fine?
If laughter leads, then all is divine.
In starlit roads where joy is near,
I'll find my way with every cheer.

Whims of an Unfinished Story

As pages turn, my tale delays,
With coffee spills in haphazard ways.
The characters dance, they laugh and play,
Missing pieces, where'd they stray?

Plot twists pop like bubble gum,
While timelines twist, a playful hum.
The hero trips over silly fates,
In raucous quest, the laughter waits.

With every draft, ideas roam,
Chasing tales of a jiggly gnome.
Stuck in plots of quirky bliss,
Each fading thought gets sealed with a kiss.

Yet penned in laughs, my heart will find,
That life's a story, sweet and blind.
In all the whims, the fun will glow,
With ink that flows, my heart will grow.

Illusions Beneath the Surface

In a world of dreams and mirage,
I search for joy in a sausage.
Yet fries seem like my only mate,
As I try to waltz with fate.

Hopping on one foot like a deer,
Stepping over balloons full of cheer.
I grasp at clouds, but they just sigh,
Oh, pizza pie, will you still fly?

The kaleidoscope shows bright hues,
Yet it's just the fridge's odd views.
Dancing around a patch of grass,
Where I trip and fall – it's quite the class!

Looking in mirrors that lie and bend,
Chasing shadows that never end.
But laughter echoes louder here,
Even when life seems unfair!

Maps of Lonesome Roads

With a map that's upside-down,
I wander through this silly town.
Left turns lead me to the mall,
While I just wanted snacks, that's all!

A compass spins just like my head,
As I search for a bed to spread.
Instead, I find a lovely tree,
Saying, "Rest your worries with me!"

Sidewalks painted in polka dots,
I stumble over my own thoughts.
Garbage cans whisper sweet nothings,
While pigeons parade with their fluffings.

Every road's a twist and shout,
As I wander without a doubt.
Though laughter leads me home tonight,
I'll take the long way for delight!

The Unseen Ladder to Nowhere

I climbed a ladder made of air,
To find a dream or some rare flair.
But each rung was a jiggling jelly,
And all I gained was a wobbly belly.

Atop the clouds, I raised a toast,
To all the dreams I love the most.
But the glasses shattered with a sneeze,
As I fell down like autumn leaves.

A rainbow peeked from out of sight,
But only offered a wobbly flight.
I landed in a pie so sweet,
With crumbs that danced around my feet.

So here I sit in this cream-filled chair,
Thinking, "What was I doing up there?"
Yet even failures bring a grin,
I'll rise again, let the fun begin!

Flickers of Hope in Dusk

As daylight fades, I light a spark,
On a birthday cake that's now a shark.
Wishes float like balloons set free,
Yet mine got stuck up in a tree.

Chasing fireflies in a silly chase,
One zipped by with a friendly face.
"Catch me if you can, oh wise old bat!"
But I just waved to that silly brat.

The stars wink down, they play it sly,
While I trip on twinkling pie.
But laughter's a beacon in the night,
With each stumble keeping spirits bright.

So here I dance beneath the sky,
With hopes that sparkle and dreams that fly.
Though the dawn may come with a sigh,
I'll greet it with giggles, oh my, oh my!

Yearning for Tomorrow's Grace

I wake up each day with a dream in my head,
But somehow my coffee has gotten too cold instead.
I search for success in my socks on the floor,
Yet the only thing found is an old rubber door.

I vision my garden with roses galore,
But the weeds seem to laugh as they take on the score.
I plot out my goals on a napkin, it's true,
Yet the only thing blooming is last night's fondue.

The cat thinks I'm nuts, but he's got it all wrong,
He lounges in sunlight while I'm singing my song.
In puddles of laughter, I tiptoe around,
Chasing dreams like a puppy not wanting to bound.

Yet I dance in my kitchen, concocting a plan,
To find what's elusive while sipping on canned.
With a sprinkle of joy and just a bit of grace,
I paint on my smile for this wild, daft race.

Echoes of Lost Possibility

Once I thought I'd fly, with a cape made of hope,
But gravity whispered, reminding my slope.
My dreams were like bubbles, so shiny and bright,
Yet they popped with a splat, like a bad food fight.

I pondered my choices, like socks in a drawer,
The left pairs with rights, but which one's the poor?
In a maze of late-night snacks, I crave the profound,
Yet I'm full of regrets that I'd rather not sound.

Perhaps I will wander through fields made of pie,
And ask for some wisdom from birds passing by.
The laughter of echoes resounds in my chest,
As I juggle my dreams like a clown at a fest.

So here's to the moments I chase with a grin,
In the carnival of life where I'm destined to spin.
While I juggle illusions and invent my own fate,
With a chuckle and two, it's never too late.

In Search of Hidden Eden

I tripped on a cloud, it was fluffy and white,
Yet somehow that cloud became more of a fright.
I stumbled and fumbled my way through the mist,
In search of a paradise, and a mad little twist.

The map in my pocket was drawn with a crayon,
And told me to find where all fun began.
But the path led to chores and an old, rusty bike,
That squeaked as it laughed with a monster-like strike.

I turned round in circles, a dizzying game,
While the squirrels held a council and whispered my name.
With nuts as their currency for wisdom to share,
I grinned at their antics, not a worry nor care.

In the chaos of dreams, I've lost track of time,
Yet I dance in the chaos, it feels so divine.
With sprinkles of laughter and dashes of fun,
My Eden exists, and it's just begun.

The Mirage of Contentment

I searched for enlightenment in a cereal bowl,
But the marshmallows laughed and stole all of my role.
I grinned at their antics, thought wisdom was near,
Yet ended up choking on last night's cold beer.

My mind is a circus, with clowns in my head,
They juggle my dreams as I lie in my bed.
The acrobats fly, while the lions just roar,
And I wave through the chaos, wanting something more.

In the quest for fulfillment, I stumble and trip,
While my wishes are tangled like fruit that won't rip.
So I'll laugh with the jesters, let nonsense unfold,
In this strange little merry-go-round, I'll be bold.

For what is contentment but finding the fun?
In the quirks and the giggles, I'll bask in the sun.
With a wink and a smile, life's silly parade,
I'll dance through the mirage, unafraid and unmade.

Distant Stars on a Cloudy Night

In the sky, a star does wink,
But my luck? It's on the brink.
Clouds parade, all dressed in gray,
Should I dance or hide away?

A shooting star, I shout, "Oh please!"
But it's too shy, just brings unease.
I try to wish on passing cars,
But they just laugh. Where are the stars?

The Weight of Untold Stories

I've got dreams like heavy bricks,
They sit around, just playing tricks.
The stories piled up to the sky,
Like laundry pegs, they just won't fly.

I try to share, but they just moan,
"Oh, not again!" they groan and groan.
In my head, they dance and jump,
But in the world, it's just a thump.

Chimeras of Contentment

I saw a unicorn on the street,
With rollerblades and shiny feet.
It offered rides to all around,
But nobody cared; just my luck found.

They say that fun is just a fright,
Like juggling ice cream in mid-flight.
Chasing dreams in silly hats,
I stumble, trip, and pet the cats.

Through the Lens of What Could Be

I wear these glasses thick as snow,
They show me paths, the places to go.
But each direction spins me 'round,
Like a pinwheel lost, I'm homeward bound.

Just peek through lenses, not for real,
And there's a world with zest and zeal.
But every time I make a change,
The view is just a little strange.

Searching for the Color of Hope

I searched high and low, in a shoe and a sock,
Found glitter and glue, but no vibrant clock.
The rainbow I sought, slipped right out of reach,
While I stumbled through puddles and aimed for the beach.

With a map made of jello, I danced on the street,
Chasing after dreams in my mismatched feet.
A kite tied to wishes, I let go with a sneeze,
Now it's caught on a cat, hanging high in the breeze.

Peeking over fences, I saw someone glow,
But they turned out to be a colorful crow.
Chickens in tutus, and cows on the run,
Oh to find hope while I'm chasing the sun!

So here's to the seekers, with paintbrush in hand,
We'll color our futures although they seem bland.
With giggles and dreams that are slightly askew,
In the search for the rainbow, let's paint ourselves blue.

The Taste of Mirages

I dreamt of a banquet, a feast full of cheer,
With chocolate fountains, and nachos right here.
But alas, it was lunch...just a cheese stick and tear,
The fries were just mirages, not a nibble to near.

I rummaged through cupboards, my hopes in a whirl,
Finding crumbs and old cookies, just a sad little pearl.
With hunger as my compass, and snacks as my goal,
I ventured for popcorn, but found just a hole.

The menu was flashy, but all that I had,
Was a wilted old salad, which made my heart sad.
So I paired it with laughter, and some fizzy old drink,
That tasted like victory — or possible sink.

So here's to the wonders found in our dreams,
Like burgers made from clouds or chocolate ice creams.
We'll hunt for each flavor, with spoons made of glee,
In the garden of mirages, we'll feast endlessly!

Compass of the Dreamer's Heart

My heart is a compass, pointy at best,
It spins round and round, never stopping for rest.
A compass for candy, for fun, and for play,
But it leads me to socks — how'd that happen today?

With directions from squirrels and maps drawn in sand,
I trek towards my dreams, though they slip from my hand.

Each turn that I take, seems to lead to a jest,
Like finding a unicorn, dressed up in a vest.

I thought it would guide me to marvelous heights,
Instead, I found pigeons, giving me sights.
The stars in my dreams lead to mismatched beds,
With pillows of popcorn, and blankets of threads.

So let's follow our hearts, with whimsy and style,
Even if we end up in a cactus in a pile.
For through giggles and fumbles, we learn as we roam,
The compass keeps spinning, and we always feel home.

In Pursuit of Fleeting Light

I chased after shadows, with hopes made of fluff,
Through gardens of giggles, where flowers are tough.
The sun winked at me, as it played hide and seek,
While I stumbled on daisies, and tripped on my cheek.

I grasped at the daylight, as it slipped out of sight,
It danced like a firefly, just taunting my plight.
With sneakers made of dreams, I raced down the lane,
But the beams of the sun just gave me a rain.

Each spark that I sought was just a silly prank,
Like socks on the line or a fish in the tank.
Yet laughs filled the air, as I chased the delight,
In this absurd adventure, I embrace the slight.

So here's to the seekers, with humor at hand,
In the pursuit of the light, we'll take a brave stand.
For fleeting and funny, all coupled in fun,
Let's savor each moment, 'til the day is done.

Lost in the Labyrinth of Aspirations

I chased my dreams around the bend,
But always tripped on my loose shoelace.
I tried to fly, but I'd just descend,
Turns out I'm not cut out for space!

With maps of glitter and plans in tow,
I boarded a train to nowhere quick.
The conductor grinned and said, "Oh no!"
I laughed, "I'll just ride this crazy trick!"

I peered through windows of lofty schemes,
Met a cat that claimed to know the way.
He purred, "Chasing dreams might be just dreams,
But aren't they better than working all day?"

So off I went with him as my guide,
Through rivers of cheese and mountains of pie.
We danced in circles, all dreams tied,
Sometimes getting lost makes you feel high!

A Journey Through the Silent Echoes

I stepped into the void of clever thought,
Where echoes laughed like silly fools.
They whispered secrets I never sought,
As I stumbled through their endless schools.

With each turn I took, I'd spin around,
Chasing shadows that were playing tricks.
I'd trip and laugh while falling to the ground,
Muttering things about failed Netflix picks.

The echoes pulled at my patient ears,
"It's easier to laugh than feel defeat!"
So I danced with doubt and all my fears,
In this silent concert, my heart skipped a beat.

Yet through the chaos, sparkles of delight,
Reminded me that joy isn't so far.
Perhaps this silly dance isn't just right,
But finding fun might be who we really are!

The Enigma of What Lies Ahead

Ah, the future—a riddle wrapped in glee,
   With clues hidden under every bed.
I sought wisdom but found lost car keys,
   And laughter instead of what I dread.

I asked a sage about fortune's game,
He chirped, "Just keep your socks on tight!"
Each answer was wild, nothing the same,
   I floated away on a kite made of light.

The path to greatness twists at odd angles,
   Like a cat chasing its own fuzzy tail.
With each puzzling turn, new wonder dangles,
   A treasure map made from a turquoise snail.

In search of the meaning beyond the mist,
   I realized the fun is in each wrong turn!
The best chase isn't the one you insist,
It's those unexpected moments that make you yearn!

The Spaces Between Heartbeats

In the pauses where time seems to freeze,
I'm thinking of cake, where is my slice?
Lost in thought, I trip on my keys,
While pondering if I roll dice.

These spaces hum with potential light,
Like the toaster waiting, it holds its breath.
Will I burn toast or make it just right?
Life's little risks shuffle cards until death.

Heartbeats echo like funky bass beats,
Ticking away as my thoughts take a dive.
I laugh at the rhythm, life's quirks and feats,
Finding joy in the odd, that's where we thrive.

So here's to the gaps, the lovely in-betweens,
Where whimsy and wonder sprinkle the air.
In each fleeting pause, dance, laugh, and glean,
For life is the fun found in places quite rare!

Glistening Wishes in the Dark

In the moonlight, I trip and fall,
Chasing dreams that seem so tall.
I tumbled just to snag a star,
But all I've caught is my pet's guitar.

With glitter bombs and silly schemes,
I package up my greatest dreams.
Yet when I open them with glee,
They pop like balloons — oh, let me be!

Half-Remembered Dreams

I had a dream I rode on bees,
Zooming past the shiny trees.
But woke up tangled in my sheets,
Wondering why my snack was peas.

I tried to train my thoughts to fly,
They took a seat and asked me why.
Oh, clever brain, you've got mad skills,
But must we always climb those hills?

A Canvas Left Blank

My brush is poised, but colors hide,
A masterpiece I can't decide.
So, I doodle squiggles on the side,
And call it 'Abstract, with Pride.'

A canvas blank, like my intent,
As I question where my time went.
Maybe I'll paint a stickman crew,
And write 'This shows my feelings too!'

Love Letters to Tomorrow

Dear Tomorrow, you fickle friend,
I write to you with love to send.
But you just giggle, make me wait,
While I munch on this cold plate.

"Where's the fun?" I often sigh,
"As moments zoom and hours fly."
You shout, "Just laugh, it's all a game!"
But I'm stuck here, calling your name!

Fragments of a Forgotten Dream

I thought I'd be a pilot, soaring high,
But here I am, just eating pie.
The clouds were calling, oh so sweet,
Instead, I'm grounded, can't find my seat.

I pictured public applause, fame galore,
But my dog just snores, and I'm stuck on the floor.
I walked the red carpet, or at least I tried,
Turns out my runway was just my backyard slide.

Chasing wild dreams on a tiny scale,
Like running a marathon, but ended up frail.
The trophy's a snack, my medal's a bite,
In the hall of fame, I'm the snack for the night.

So here's to the dreams that float far away,
Like balloons in the breeze, they've led me astray.
I'll keep on dreaming, it's really no crime,
While munching on chips, and sipping on lime.

The Road Not Taken

I stood at a crossroads, which way to go?
One path was bright, the other a no-show.
I chose the one with a sign for snacks,
   But ended up lost in a field of flax.

There were whispers of fortune, some said I'd win,
But I tripped on a rock and fell in a bin.
I took the wrong turn; they said I was bold,
Now I'm selling lemonade in the hot sun, sold!

They promised adventure, excitement, and thrill,
But here I am stuck, taking care of a grill.
I wave at the travelers, oh what a sight,
While I flip my burgers, they're soaring in flight.

So here's to choices, both funny and wry,
My road's not glamorous, but I can still fry.
A cook in the kitchen, I call it my fate,
In this life's little circus, I'm the master of plate.

Uncharted Paths of Ambition

A map in my head, marked 'success' in red,
But here I am, lost in a field of bread.
I wanted to conquer, climb mountains so steep,
But I've settled for snacks, in my comfy chair, sleep.

I dreamed of a mansion, a yacht on the sea,
Now it's a couch and a cat sipping tea.
Life threw me curveballs, I dodged them with flair,
Yet all that I caught was a sock from the air.

I'm painting my dreams with the brushes of fun,
Though some days I'm more 'meh' than a shiny pun.
With laughter as fuel, and giggles as glue,
I craft my existence, it's quite the brew.

So here's to the journeys, absurd and absurd,
The pathways that wander, and dreams that get blurred.
With the humor of life, and a wink in my eye,
I'll dance through the chaos, like a pie in July.

Whispers of a Distant Joy

I once sought a life filled with laughter and cheer,
But now I just chuckle when I spill my beer.
The joy that I chased, all glitter and gold,
Turns out it's just tales that my grandma once told.

A ride on a unicorn, oh wouldn't that be great?
Instead, I ride buses, always running late.
The stars were my limits, the skies were my guide,
Now I count ceiling tiles when I'm stuck inside.

I yearned for the glitz, the glamour, the fame,
Yet I'm happy with crumbs from my cat's fancy game.
The sparkle I dreamed of is just dust in the air,
We're all just pretenders with wild styles to wear.

So here's to the whispers, those giggles and sighs,
I'll find joy in the mess, beneath all these lies.
With a sprinkle of humor and a dollop of cheer,
I'll treasure each moment, the good and the sheer.

Embracing the Whisper of Possibility

I wandered through a forest of dreams,
Where squirrels wore suits and plotted schemes.
They whispered secrets of what could be,
While I tripped over my own two feet.

A fish in a tux, he winked at me,
Said, "Dance with the stars, it's wild and free!"
I tried to boogie but hit a tree,
Then laughed at the way life let me be.

In a world where pigeons play chess,
And my ice cream always says, "I guess!"
I chased a rainbow, slipped in the goo,
But at least I'm smiling, how 'bout you?

So let's toast to dreams, both weird and grand,
With unicorns serving drinks from their hand.
In this quirky life, I must confess,
I thrive on the chaos, it's truly the best!

Heartstrings Tethered to Impossibility

My heartstrings dance like spaghetti on a plate,
Tangled in knots, oh, isn't that great!
I tried to unravel, but what did I find?
A portal to nowhere, my mind in a bind.

A cat with a monocle sipped on his tea,
He said, "Life's a joke! Come laugh with me!"
So I joined the circus of thoughts that I chase,
And learned to juggle my socks in disgrace.

In a parallel universe of whims and chance,
Where penguins wear ties and hippos can dance.
I stumbled through portals of silly delight,
With llamas in tutus and kites taking flight.

So here's to the heartstrings, forever askew,
Playing tunes of the silly, both old and new.
In this realm of mischief, I twirl and I sway,
With giggles and hiccups, I'll find my way!

Undreamt Dreamscapes

In lands of unsleeping where llamas take flight,
I tried to catch clouds, but they slipped out of sight.
The moon offered donuts, sweet glazed and round,
But I fell in a marshmallow pit on the ground.

With sprinkles on top, the mountains I climbed,
Once slipped on some jelly, and oh boy, I rhymed.
A frog in a top hat proposed a fine tea,
I turned down the offer, 'twas too fancy for me.

In gardens of rainbows where shadows look bright,
The flowers all giggled at passers each night.
I danced with a pickle, we twirled in the breeze,
While squirrels took selfies with ease, if you please!

So let's paint our wishes with laughter and cheers,
In a world where the quirky dissolves all our fears.
For here in these dreamscapes, absurd and profound,
We find space for laughter where joy can abound!

Where the Wild Wishes Roam

In a field full of wishes, I lost my marbles,
A cow rode a bicycle, doing some garbles.
I chased after dreams on a pogo stick,
While fish told me jokes that landed quite thick.

The sky wore a tutu, all flutter and flair,
As kangaroos practiced their ballet in air.
I joined in their dance, but my feet felt like glue,
While dreams whispered softly, "Just be true to you!"

A dragon played cards with the clouds up above,
He challenged my heart to a game of sweet love.
I folded my fears, tossed doubt to the wind,
And laughed as the wild wishes jumped and grinned.

So let's spin our tales on this merry-go-round,
Where laughter and whimsy are always found.
In the land of the wishing, let's live without care,
For each wild adventure leads us to share!

Dance of the Unfulfilled

In a room of socks and old regrets,
I twirl in circles like a pet rock.
My dreams have legs but lack the bets,
They dance on floors—where's my clock?

I trip on hopes, laugh out loud,
As wishes float on pancakes wide.
My goals are meek, my dreams too proud,
But hey, I've got this clownish stride.

I check my closet, find what's lost,
A sweater labeled 'Do Not Wear.'
My priorities come at a cost,
Still, I embrace my crazy flair.

With a shimmy and a shake of might,
I'll groove through walls of every doubt.
If rhythm fails, I'll just ignite,
An absurd dance that's all about!

Catching Ghosts in the Wind

I run with nets beneath the stars,
Chasing breezes that giggle and tease.
My ambitions hover, like wayward cars,
Zooming past like whispers in trees.

A gust of dreams? I'll take a bite!
Yet all I catch is a balmy sigh.
Wandering in shadows, quite the sight,
I pretend I'm sprightly—oh me, oh my!

Each breeze I chase is like a joke,
Tickling hopes with a flick of fate.
One day, I'll catch that big old cloak,
And wear it proud till I find my mate.

But for now, I'll skip and spin,
With spirits dancing in my chest.
Who knew that laughter hides within,
These fleeting whispers turned to jest!

Behind the Veil of Now

In a bubble of 'what might have been,'
I sip on tea brewed from lost dreams.
Life in the future feels like a sin,
While here I am, or so it seems.

I brew my plans in rainbow hues,
With sprinkles of doubt and a twist of fate.
Each choice is tricky; the path can confuse,
Yet here I am, contemplating my plate.

Behind the curtain, a dance unfolds,
With marionettes dressed in silly acts.
I pull the strings to watch as they mold,
While snacking on popcorn and laughing in packs.

So let's toast to the moments we miss,
And juggle our hopes like balls of yarn.
Life's a riddle wrapped in a kiss,
While we wade through chaos—life is our charm!

Heartbeats in a Distant Land

I trek through fields where dreams begin,
With heartbeats thumping like heavy bass.
Searching for laughter, oh where have you been?
In a distance that feels like outer space.

Each step's a giggle—I'm lost in thought,
As shadows linger trying to tease.
Misfit ambitions are all I've got,
Juggling wishes like a playful breeze.

From the corner of my eye, I see,
A mirage dancing on the setting sun.
It winks at me, then runs with glee,
While I'm here stuck—oh boy, this is fun!

So I'll march on, life's paneled maze,
With laughter echoing in the air.
For even if I spiral in a daze,
What matters most? I'm still aware!

Roads Less Traveled

I took a left where others go right,
A shortcut to nowhere, what a strange sight.
GPS says 'rerouting' with a sigh,
But honestly, I think I could fly.

I met a cow who gave me a grin,
She said, 'Chasing dreams is where to begin.'
Milk your desires, let them all flow,
But watch where you step; there's mud below!

The street signs are laughing, how rude,
With arrows and hearts, and one that says 'food.'
I dance with the hedges, I sing with the trees,
Where's the legible map? Oh, just a tease!

Yet here in the chaos, I find my delight,
With giggles of gnomes as my guiding light.
Each twist and turn writes an unfolding tale,
Of adventures unwritten, a grand happy fail.

Hearts Untamed

My heart's on a leash, but it won't obey,
It pants like a puppy, wanting to play.
'No chasing squirrels!' it hears me shout,
But watch it go—zooming about!

It bumps into wishes, then takes them for snacks,
While I sit with a latte, plotting my tracks.
'Stay in your lane!' I mentally plead,
But off it runs, following a bead.

The neighbors just chuckle at my wild heart's race,
As it chases stars through outer space.
Jumping on clouds, it's quite the spry flake,
Who knew desires could waltz and partake?

Yet, I can't deny it's quite the fair fight,
With reckless abandon and sheer delight.
My heart's like a toddler, no doubt it will roam,
But that's how it makes this chaos feel like home.

A Symphony of Forgotten Wishes

Once jotted on napkins, dreams began to hum,
Conducted by a cat who strummed a drum.
Each wish a note, floating through air,
While my laundry spins like it just doesn't care.

Forgotten melodies, on kitchen countertops,
Dancing with dust, playing hopscotch with crops.
'Hey, don't quit your daydreams!' they sing and they cheer,
As spaghetti sways like it owns the frontier.

The stove starts to whistle a tune of delight,
While my pets join the chorus—what a wild sight!
They twirl on the carpet, they pounce with finesse,
Making dinner prep seem like a grand, crazy mess.

So here we compose in this mayhem of glee,
With spoons as our batons, chasing wild jubilee.
Each wish is a rhythm, and life's just a song,
In the symphony of laughter, where all folks belong.

Sketches of What Could Be

I doodled a dream on the back of my hand,
A castle of pancakes, oh how it would stand!
With syrupy rivers and whipped cream galore,
I'm the king of this breakfast, forever and more.

But then reality called from the fridge,
Saying, 'You'll need eggs; let's not scrimp!'
So I gathered my crayons, ready to draw,
A world made of laughter and an ice cream law.

Sketching adventures while sipping my tea,
Croquet with lobsters, let's make them agree.
A picnic with penguins on a hot summer's day,
With sunscreen and flip-flops—who would take that away?

Yet through imagination's flight, I see,
That even small doodles can dance and run free.
So here's to the scribbles, the what-might-have-beens,
For life's a canvas where daydreaming wins.

Beyond the Walls of Reality

Peeking through portals to worlds yet unseen,
Where socks speak in riddles, and slippers are keen.
A realm where my cat dons a top hat and bow,
As stars binge-watch sitcoms in their cosmic show.

I slip through the curtains of mundane and gray,
To chaos where jellybeans lead the way.
With rules that are floppy and time that stands still,
And pizza that always fulfills the thrill.

Adventures unravel, like yarn in a race,
While toasters are wizards, each slice finds its place.
My shoes do a jig, giving rhythm to luck,
As unicorns frolic in a vast bubble truck.

So here I reside, 'neath the sun and the moon,
In worlds where reality's not in the room.
With laughter as my compass, I wander with glee,
For beyond these walls, oh, how wild life can be!

Fleeting Shadows of Desire

I chased a dream on roller skates,
But tripped on hopes, oh, what a fate!
With ice cream cones and sprinkles bright,
I laughed so hard, I lost my sight.

A unicorn made of marshmallow,
Promised gold and a real good show.
But all I got was bubblegum,
And clowns that made my heart go numb.

I built a castle made of cheese,
Inviting friends, oh, what a tease!
But mice threw parties in the night,
And left me with a cheesy fright.

So here I sit, with dreams so wild,
A jester's heart of a foolish child.
In shadows cast, I'll dance and play,
For laughter lifts those blues away.

Dreams just out of Reach

I had a goal to touch the stars,
But fell in mud while riding cars.
Sipping soda, dreaming big,
Yet tripped on a tiny, dancing pig.

The prize was sweet, a golden crown,
But it rolled away, oh, what a clown!
Chasing it through fields of green,
I found instead a tiny bean.

I tried to fly with wings of dreams,
But tangled up in ruffled seams.
A bird chuckled from a tree,
As I landed near a buzzing bee.

Yet here I am, still full of cheer,
With donut holes and root beer near.
For every stumble, every fall,
Is just a chance to laugh through it all.

Echoes of a Path Untaken

I walked a road of twinkling lights,
Hoping for adventures, grand delights.
But all I found were feet and shoes,
That danced right past, with silly moves.

I tried to gallop like a horse,
But ended up on a wild course.
With rubber chickens in my bag,
And socks that smelled, oh what a drag!

I sought a map, all filled with gold,
But found instead a tale retold.
Of here and there, and right and wrong,
But hey, I've still got my silly song.

So off I go, on roads unknown,
With laughter as my heart's true throne.
For every twist, another guess,
Is truly life's delightful mess.

Whispers of a Forgotten Journey

A suitcase filled with hopes and dreams,
Was left behind—it's bursting at the seams.
With travel plans on napkin scraps,
And tales of ghouls and funny mishaps.

I boarded trains that went nowhere fast,
With snacks that squeaked and friendships cast.
The sun went down, my map went haywire,
A cozy bus turned into a tire fire.

I wandered through a land of socks,
Where every door require an ox.
I climbed a tree to see the sights,
But only met some fuzzy mites.

Now here I stand, with tales to share,
Of wibbly wobblies and the dragon's lair.
Though routes may twist and laughter reign,
The whispers guide me home again.

www.ingramcontent.com/pod-product-compliance
Lightning Source LLC
Chambersburg PA
CBHW071845160426
43209CB00003B/426